D1528947

LOVE RULES

Andrea Melvin,
Dave Eaton, and
Michael Clark Jr.

illustrated by
**Danielle
Parchment**

Feiwel & Friends
New York

A Feiwel and Friends Book

An imprint of Macmillan Publishing Group, LLC

120 Broadway, New York, NY 10271 • mackids.com

Our books may be purchased in bulk for promotional, educational, or business use.
Please contact your local bookseller or the Macmillan Corporate and Premium Sales Department
at (800) 221-7945 ext. 5442 or by email at MacmillanSpecialMarkets@macmillan.com.

Library of Congress Cataloging-in-Publication Data is available.

First edition, 2022

Book design by Cindy De la Cruz

Feiwel and Friends logo designed by Filomena Tuosto

Printed in China by RR Donnelley Asia Printing Solutions Ltd.,
Dongguan City, Guangdong Province

ISBN 978-1-250-78056-0

1 3 5 7 9 10 8 6 4 2

Dedicated to the friends, social workers,
and teachers who change so many kids' lives

It was time to leave.

Again.

As he'd done before, Michael packed his bag and carried with him many questions.

Where are we going?

Who will be there?

Will they have macaroni
and cheese?

Hand in hand, they walked.

As he looked up ahead,
he thought about what he'd left behind.

His tummy squeezed.
A last question whispered,

Will I stay?

Twinkly eyes and warm smiles he'd never met before welcomed him in.

"Hello, Michael. We made you macaroni and cheese. We hope you like it," said Andrea and Dave.

"How did you know that was my favorite?" he asked.

Michael explored the pictures on the wall.

"Who is that? And that?"

"That is our family, Michael."

He clutched his bag.

"Would you like to play with Rory?"

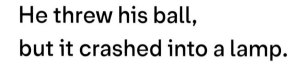

He threw his ball, but it crashed into a lamp.

Oh no, he worried. *Do I have to leave?*

But Dave reached out his hand.

"Don't worry about that, Michael. Come. Let's go see your room."

"*My* room?"

Michael packed his days with new adventures.

One night, he camped out under the stars for the first time.

As school approached, he carried with him many more questions.

Where is my new school?

Who is going to take me?

Will they have chicken nuggets?

On his first day, they walked him up the steps to his classroom.

Michael's tummy squeezed. A last question whispered, *Will I belong?*

Looking around, he saw new faces.

"Do I look different from the other kids?" Michael asked.

"You do, and we are all unique in our own ways," said Andrea.

"And the kids can't wait to meet you," said the teacher.

Michael had new rules to learn, too. Some of those rules were hard at first.

He forgot to raise his hand.

He couldn't stay in his seat.

Taking turns was tricky.

One day, his wiggles grew rambunctious and the teacher had a talk with him.

Oh no, he worried. *Do I have to leave?*

"We are all learning here," she said.
"Let's try again."

But Michael sat alone.

Just then, he felt a hand reach out.

And another.

And another.

His classmates surrounded him.

He felt like they were holding his heart in their hands.

He welcomed every face.

"Hi, I'm Michael. Do you want to be best friends?"

They giggled under the parachute.

They whispered during naptime.

When Lily lost her crayon, Michael shared his.

Will this feeling be forever?

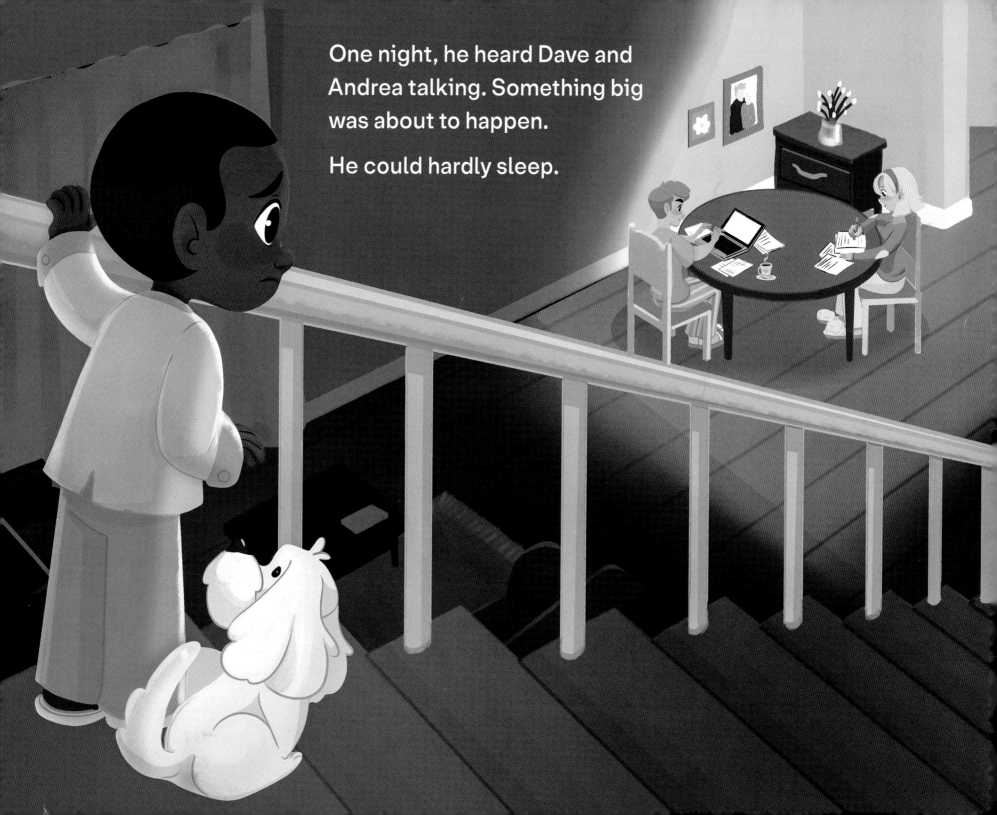

One night, he heard Dave and Andrea talking. Something big was about to happen.

He could hardly sleep.

The next morning, he packed his belly with pancakes.
He was bursting with questions.

Where are we going?

Who will be there?

Will you—

But before he could ask,
he was swept out the door.

Hand in hand in hand, they walked up the street to the courthouse.

His stomach squeezed. His last question finally whispered,
Will you . . . be my forever family?

But as soon as Michael entered the courtroom, he didn't just know the answer . . .

He felt it.

He felt it from the judge sitting in front of him.

He felt it from his mom and dad by his side.

He felt it from the twenty-one hearts glued on rulers, waving behind him.

"LOVE RULES!" cheered his classmates.

Yet nothing could truly measure the love Michael felt in his heart.

"I'm adopted!"

For forever and always,
Michael was home.

Michael was a friend.
Michael was family.

And Michael never heard those questions whispered again.

PICTURES OF A FOREVER FAMILY!

Based on a true story that captured the hearts of many as their courtroom adoption video went viral, Michael, Andrea, and Dave tell the story of opening your hearts to one another.

Andrea, Michael, and Rory cuddling when Michael first arrives.

Family photo in Grand Rapids, Michigan.

Michael and Rory becoming fast friends.

Michael and Dave on the first day of school.

Michael enjoying a camping adventure!